ANCIENT GREECE
A CONCISE & ILLUSTRATED HISTORY

ATHENS
ΠΛΕΙΑΔΕΣ

ANCIENT GREECE
A CONCISE AND ILLUSTRATED HISTORY
Copyright Philip Katsaros
ISBN: 978-960-90970-2-4

ENGLISH TRANSLATION REVISED BY DIOGENES LALLOS
IN GREEK REVISED BY KATERINA ANTONIOU AND VASSILIKI MORAITI
DIGITAL PROCESSING BY CHRISANTHI RETSOU
TEXT-ILLUSTRATION: PHILIP KATSAROS

CONTENTS

PREHISTORIC YEARS
HISTORIC YEARS
ATHENS AND THE BIRTH OF DEMOCRACY
MEDIAN WARS
PROSPERITY AND HEGEMONY OF ATHENS
PELOPONNESIAN WAR
THE PRIME OF MACEDONIA AND PHILIP B
ALEXANDER THE GREAT
HELLENISTIC PERIOD

KNOSSOS

PREHISTORIC YEARS

The first Hellenic civilizations evolved before 5.000 B.C in large parts of the Hellenic regions. It was a geographically gifted land with the four seasons of the year well-defined, profuse and multifarious vegetation, fabulous landscapes, exquisite land terrain and hundreds of islands.

This was a suitable environment for the development of the following civilizations:
The proto-Minoan (in Crete), the proto-Hellenic, (in the mainland of Hellas), the proto-Cycladic, (with Cyclades as the epicenter, also famous for the Cycladic statuettes), and the civilization of the northern and eastern Aegean Sea islands.

These civilizations coexisted and prospered harmoniously for the longest period of the 3rd millennium. The Minoan civilization evolved in Crete from 5.000 B.C and reached its peak in the middle of the 16th century B.C with Knossos as the epicenter. Later, at the opposite side of the island, Festus also reached the peak of its power.

The Cretans developed the arts, the trade and dominated the seas. The palaces of Knossos were big and luxurious. They occupied an area of 22.000 square meters, with many floors, arcades and courtyards. Furthermore they had perfect hydraulic installations, draining systems, baths, ceremony halls, guest rooms and more.

The masterly wall-paintings, give us an idea of their bright multi-colored lives.

Later, from 1600 B.C to 1100 B.C significant civilizations are being developed in Peloponnese, Argos, Tirynthus and Mycenae. Especially the power and wealth of the Mycenae kings were monumental and their reputation spread in many parts of Hellas. (The king of Mycenae Agamemnon is famous from the Homeric epics). It remained in History as the Mycenean civilization.

ACROPOLIS OF MYCENAE

Orpheus Hesiod Homer Aristarchus Solon
Democritus Heraclitus Pythagoras

In the book the term GREEK is replace by the original word "HELLENE" also the word GREECE is replaced by the word "HELLAS".

HISTORIC YEARS

Since the 8th century B.C personalities or factions from the Hellenic cities took the initiative to set off, explore and colonize other territories. Thus during the 7th and 6th century B.C there were hundreds of Hellenic kingdoms and city-states in Metropolitan Hellas (which includes the geographic regions of Peloponnese, Sterea Hellas, Crete, Thessaly, Macedonia, Epirus, Thrace, islands of the Aegean and Ionian Sea), Cyprus, Asia Minor coastline – the Ionian coalition formed of twelve united cities (dodecapolis) was famous - the coastline of the Black Sea, south Italy and Sicily – known as "Great Hellas" – and in small regions of north Africa, south France and southeast Spain. (The Hellenic lands shown on the map are tinged with orange).

The ancient Hellenic civilization had already started to evolve. Before the 9th century B.C the names of bards Orpheus, Dimodokos and Phemius are mentioned.

In the 9th century B.C the great poet Homer (from the Ionian coastline) gave us the masterly heroic epics "Iliad" and "Odyssey".

In the 8th century B.C Hesiod gave us the famous didactic epics "Deeds and days" and "Theogony". In the 7th and 6th century B.C, the Hellenes laid the life-giving foundations of philosophy and science. Thus the chain reaction of the continuous expansion of sciences and knowledge started and continues to the present day.

The wise men, the mathematicians, physicians and engineers of the era were many and some of them were: Xenophantes (570-475) B.C, Thales from Miletus (624-546) B.C, Pittakos from Mitylene, Vias from Priene, Solon the Athenian, Cleovoulos from Rhodes, Chilon the Lacedaemonian, Periandros the Corinthian, Anaximander (611-546) B.C, Anaximenes (585-525), Heraclitus (544-484) B.C, Pythagoras the Samian (570-496), Parmenides (550-470), Zeno the Eleatic (498-429), Empedocles, Anaxagoras, Democritus, Aesculapius, Ippodamos (5th century B.C), Epimenides the Cretan (7th-6th century B.C) and others.

An important parameter for the development of the ancient Hellenic civilization was also the Hellenic language, which complies with a mathematical structure, has liveliness and the capacity to regenerate new words in order to convey new concepts.

ATHENS AND THE BIRTH OF DEMOCRACY

The first inhabitants of Attica were farmers and stock-breeders yet they also tried to find products outside their country so they built ships and became remarkable mariners and traders. The last king of Athens was Codrus. Since 684 B.C 9 sovereign rulers were elected from the aristocracy. With the establishment of coins as a medium for exchange, the local agricultural products lost their value in comparison to the cheaper products that the traders were bringing in from other places. Thus the farmers started borrowing money from the noblemen at the risk of losing their properties.

That brought about an opposition towards the noblemen. The mariners and tradesmen sided with the farmers as their social status was constantly improving and they could no longer bear the aristocracy's privileges. Therefore, the pressure of events brought about new decrees. For the first time, Dragon puts forward written laws, which were know in History for their rigor. Later on, Solon (594) composes righteous laws, reconciles the opposition of classes and succeeds in saving the farmer's properties from the noblemen. From 561 to 510 Pisistratus and his sons ruled Athens.

Subsequently Clisthenes prevails who laid the foundations of the Athenian democracy. Clisthenes divided Attica in 10 tribes, each tribe consisted of 10 municipalities (100 municipalities). Every tribe would elect 50 representatives and as a result the Parliament consisted of 500 representatives. By now the Parliament together with the "assembly of the people" ruled and the Athenians were citizens who had equal rights among them.

The Parliament would elect the president and the governmental committee per appointed time periods. All the free citizens participated in those assemblies. The "assembly of the people" was the meeting that took place regularly in order to debate about serious issues (for the strategic and political activities of Athens, for the election of general, for the trade, for the state expenditure and others) and to make final decisions by voting.

Hellenic cities of ASIA MINOR (IONIAN CITIES) : Miletus, Ephesus, Teos, Alicarnassos, Priene, Clazomene, Smyrna and others.
Cities of GREAT HELLAS (Southern Italy and sicily) : Taras, Syracuse, Selinounte, Elea, Neptunian, Cyme, Crotona, Pigion and others.
Cities of METROPOLITAN HELLAS: Sparta, Athens, Argos, Pella, Thebes, Aigai, Olynth, Mantineia, Tegea, Corinth, dodona, Ambrakia and others.
Hellenic cities in the Agean and Ionian islands were simultaneously flourishing.

MEDIAN WARS

Solon once arrived in Sardinia, invited by King Croesus. In order to impress him, the King flaunted his riches and asked him if he knew of any person happier than him. Solon replied that he knew of a citizen Tello who was virtuous, creative and diligent, he had many well-behaved children, and led a life without deprivations and fell gloriously fighting for his country.

Croesus, asked him again. Solon, replied that he knew Vitona and Cleovi whose hearts were full of family love. When one day the oxen couldn't carry the carriage, the two brothers yoked their bodies to it and took their mother to Hera's temple. Croesus then angrily said to him: "So, you do not regard us as happy people?!"

Solon replied: "King of Lydians, God endowed the Hellenes with moderation and wisdom with modesty but without impudence...

We Hellenes regard as true happy people those whom God has helped to preserve their happiness till the end of their lives despite the constant changes in their life-time... Otherwise it's like declaring winner an athlete who is still competing...."

Years later, when Croesus was defeated by Cyrus (king of Persians), he was dragged bound in chains before Cyrus. Thereupon, Croesus cried out three times: "Oh Solon!"

Cyrus was puzzled and asked him if he had called the name of a man or a god. Then Croesus told him the story and the words of Solon...

Cyrus remained thoughtful for some time and understanding the moral of the story, set Croesus free and honored him! In this way, Solon with his words, saved a king and taught a lesson to another. That king was Cyrus the Great (559-528), the king of Persians, who laid the foundations of the Persian Empire. He subjugated the Median kingdom, the Babylonians, the Ionian cities of the Asia Minor coastline (despite the severe urge of Sparta not to harm the Hellenic cities) and reached the borders of Egypt which was also conquered by his son Camvyses in 525 B.C.

After Camvyses, Darius A' the Great reigned, who organized and civilized his state and helped the flourishing of the trade. (In his court, he invites the best Hellene engineers, doctors and artists). In 517 he subjugated Samos and its strong fleet. In 515 he defeats the Scythians and the Thracians. He joins forces with the Phoenician fleet and becomes the ruler of the Aegean Sea. At that period, the Persian kingdom expanded from Carthage to Indies and from Bosporus to Abyssinia. Never before had such an Empire emerged, with vast expanses, powerful organization and invincible army (it is shown on the map with tints of green). By now, the Persian kings want to subjugate the last free places of the known ancient world, the Hellenic kingdoms and city-states of the west which conduct trade from the Mediterranean to the Black Sea. It won't take long for the pretent to arise...

In 499 B.C the Hellenic cities of the Asia Minor coastline rise in revolt (Ionian revolution).

For the first time in their history the Persians confront the national resistance of one nation. They mobilize military forces on land and sea and after hard-fought struggles that lasted 5 years they manage to overpower it.

During the duration of the revolution, Athens and Eretria sent support to the Ionian cities with 20 and 5 trireme ships respectively. That event would be the occasion that the Persians were looking for in order to march out against the Hellenes of the West...

493 B.C
Filaides Miltiades, leaves his fields in Thrace and returns to Athens, where he earns the title of one of the ten (10) generals.

Miltiades! Miletus, the jewel of the Ionian cities, has finally been besieged by the Persian fleet and strong land forces. The Ionian revolution wore away...

Thales from Miletus, foresaw the Persian threat and suggested the Ionian alliance, but he was ignored. The Ionian alliance was formed later, with Panionios in Mycali as its center. Mistakes and misunderstandings during the duration of the revolution cost us. Nevertheless, the Persians now have the opportunity they were looking for.

492 B.C
Darius, king of the Persian Empire had already began preparing his troops. He had ordered one of his servants to remind him daily: "Master, do not forget the Athenians". (Because of the reinforcements that Athens had sent to the Ionian cities).

Master Darius, according to your orders, the set-up of the expeditionary force is complete. The fleet composed of 600 ships is ready to sail.

PRIENE

The winter came early. The Persian fleet met with an unprecedented storm in the coastline of Strimonikos Bay! Half of the ships were destroyed and Mardonios returned to base.

Darius was not discouraged. He gave orders for the preparation of new forces and entrusted the leadership to Dates who was competent in naval operations and his nephew Artaphernes.

CORFU

The Athenians decided to repulse the Persian invasion. They sent messengers to the Spartan leaders of the Peloponnesian alliance for reinforcements.

Sparta, the strongest Hellenic state, responded to their first appeal. They took hostages from Aegina and performed a military demonstration against Argos, in order to force them into upholding neutrality.

The summer of 490 B.C the Persian fleet crosses the Aegean. After they desolated Eretria, they stationed themselves at Marathon in Attica.

ATHENS

The messenger Phidippides has arrived from Sparta, he should present himself to the generals' council.

The Spartans will come to our assistance with 2.000 soldiers, yet they sent us a message to wait till the full moon.

With this Spartan force supporting us we will be stronger however this delay may turn out to be catastrophic.

We can confront the Persians without any external help!

But, Miltiades, up to the present day there is no army that has confronted the Persians victoriously in an open plain.

The Persian army has more than 80.000 men while our forces are not more than 10.000 soldiers together with the 1.000 Plataens who have come for reinforcement.

You are right... The Persian Empire has enslaved more than 40 different nations. They have unlimited financial resources and strong and skillful troops. However, do not forget that I know the way they fight.

Their army is deployed by situating a large number of select soldiers in the center of the battle array while forming a sparse deployment on the flanks. If we position sparse and select deployment in the center and more compact on the flanks, we will then engage in a battle array front length, equal to the Persian, thus avoiding the encirclement and giving us the chance to close in upon them.

The Athenian generals agreed with Miltiades' suggestion and war lord Kallimahos (Commander- in – Chief of the Athenians) gave the signal for departure to Marathon.

Our scouts saw the Hellenic army approaching. Muster all our men!

During September 490 the legendary battle of Marathon takes place.

The Persian center is pressing the Athenian center en masse cousing it to retreat, but the Athenians fight bravely and keep the battle under control...

On the contrary, the Athenian flanks knock down the Persians who begin to retreat. The Athenian deployment takes the shape of a half-moon closing in upon the Persians.

The Persians realize the encirclement and panic. With battle cries their full force opens up a road towards the ships while the Athenians are chasing them.

With serious losses and with great difficulty, the majority of their army embarked and set sail......

It was noon already, when an Athenian soldier left and ran to his city. He wanted to be the first to bring the message of victory to his hometown. He arrived exhausted and just before he passed away he shouted the good tidings before the deans. He was happy, he had accomplished his goal.

In order to honor him, the civilized world made his achievement into an athletic tradition, the Marathon run.

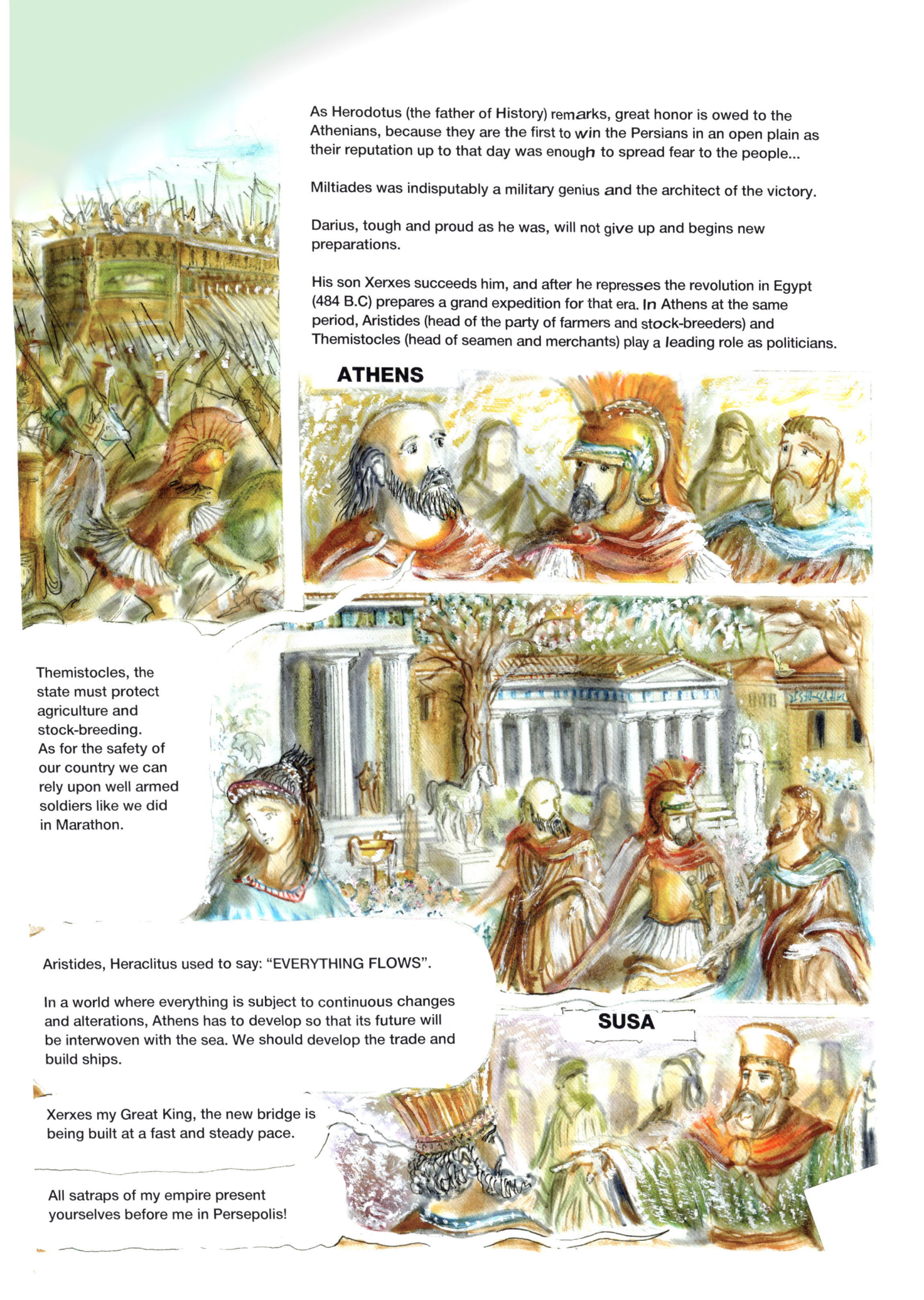

As Herodotus (the father of History) remarks, great honor is owed to the Athenians, because they are the first to win the Persians in an open plain as their reputation up to that day was enough to spread fear to the people...

Miltiades was indisputably a military genius and the architect of the victory.

Darius, tough and proud as he was, will not give up and begins new preparations.

His son Xerxes succeeds him, and after he represses the revolution in Egypt (484 B.C) prepares a grand expedition for that era. In Athens at the same period, Aristides (head of the party of farmers and stock-breeders) and Themistocles (head of seamen and merchants) play a leading role as politicians.

ATHENS

Themistocles, the state must protect agriculture and stock-breeding. As for the safety of our country we can rely upon well armed soldiers like we did in Marathon.

Aristides, Heraclitus used to say: "EVERYTHING FLOWS".

In a world where everything is subject to continuous changes and alterations, Athens has to develop so that its future will be interwoven with the sea. We should develop the trade and build ships.

SUSA

Xerxes my Great King, the new bridge is being built at a fast and steady pace.

All satraps of my empire present yourselves before me in Persepolis!

EPHESUS

This is period is extremely critical... Carthage is getting ready to attack the cities of great Hellas. Simultaneously the Imposing campaign, of the Persians against Athens and any other Hellenic city that will pose resistance, is imminent. Xerxes is gathering soldiers from all the people of his empire, and will oblige the hellenic cities of Asia Minor to provide ships and soldiers for his forces.

If all of us Hellenes were united, we would be able to directly face any attack much easier. However every city has its own goverment, therefore it is difficult for us to work together, and sometimes we are led to civil wars.

The Persian army and fleet are moving parallel to the coastline....They cross Thrace, advance into Macedonia and stream to Thessaly. From wherever they cross, the wells dry up and the crops get destroyed....

The king of Macedonia has been taken hostage by the Persians!

The Persians camped in front of Thermopylae. Xerxes waited 4 days as he believed Leonidas would hesitate at the large number of his troops and finally surrender. However this did not occur...

They were afraid they might get encircled by the Macedonians while advancing into Southern Hellas.

Herodotus writes for Xerxes' army: "Someone could see in Xerxes' army, Persians, Medes, Hyrcanians and Parthians with tiaras and varicolored greatcoats, their crossbows and woven shields.

Assyrians with bronze helmets, wooden clubs and javelins. Sacians with pointed caps, bows and hoes. Caspians with clothes from goat-hair, cane bows and scimitars. Indians with cotton clothes and bows from Indian cane. Arabs with loose robes and gibbous long bows. Ethiopians dressed with skins from panthers and lions and their bodies smeared with cast and ink, with their long bows made of palm twigs.

Ethiopians of Asia, who wore horse-skins on their heads with the mane thrown over and the ears erect. Laves dressed with skins. Lydians armed liked the Hellenes. Thrace from Bithynia, who wore fox-skin on their heads ..." (Herodotus Z', 61)

Master, the small Hellenic army shows no sign of commotion. On the contrary, peace and unity prevail.

Send deputation to their general!

At the same time the Hellenic fleet is getting ready to intercept the Persian ships.

King Leonidas, Xerxes, Lord of the Persian Empire, offers you the opportunity to return back to your homes alive, if only you hand over your weapons!

THERMOPYLAE

COME AND GET THEM!

After Leonidas' laconic reply the deputation left. Then someone spoke once again to the hoplites and the Spartan Diemekes replied to him.

Why do you take the decision for such a difficult battle, when our archers throw their arrows they will shade the sun!

Good. Then we will have our battle in the shade.

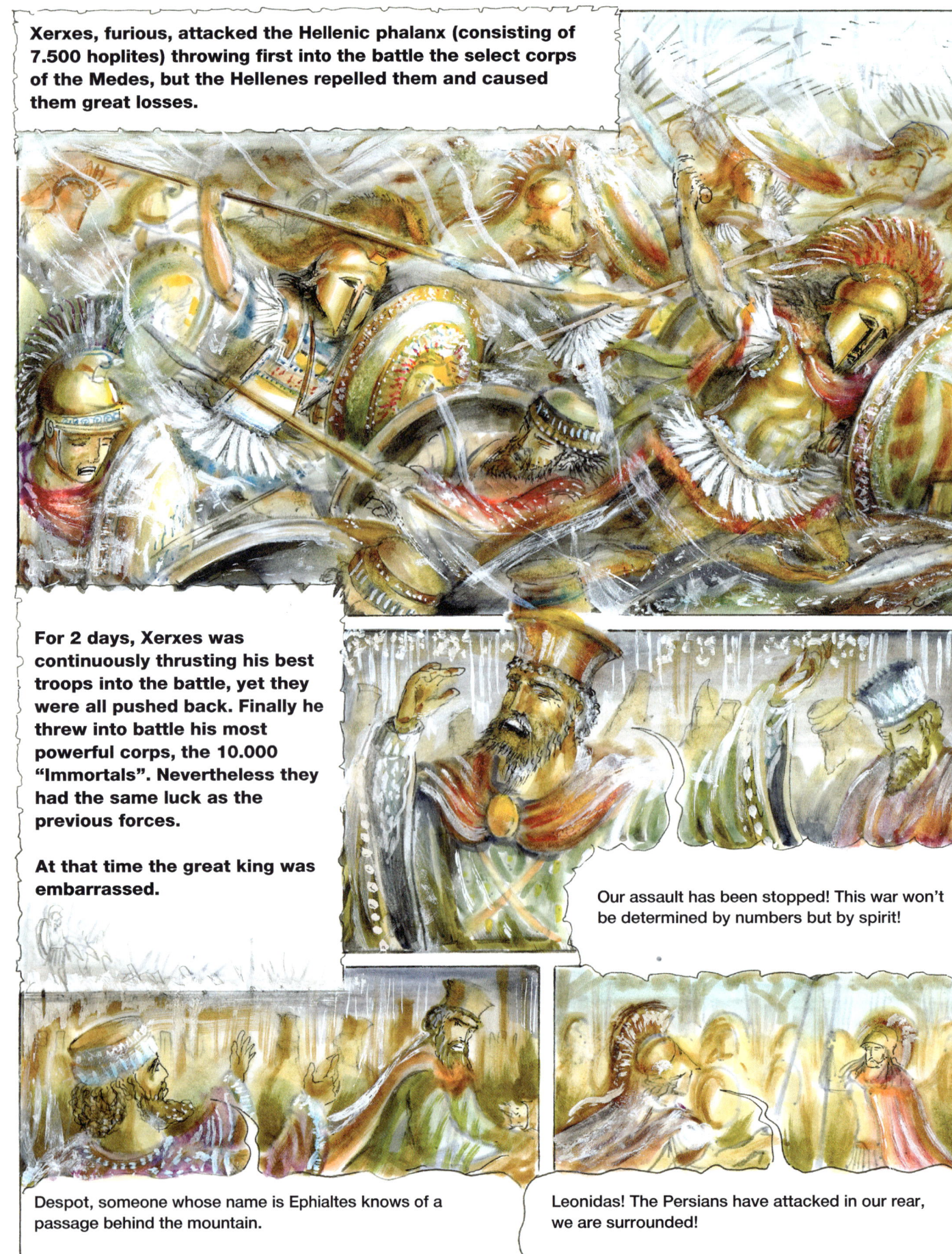

Leonidas realizing the consequences of the encirclement, ordered the generals of the Hellenic cities to muster their hoplites and leave so that they can be helpful for future battles.

Leonidas with his 300 Spartans remained to defend their withdrawal. With him 700 Thespians, also stayed who did not want to obey him...

These 1.000 lions were encircled by the immense Persian army. The unknown up to now land of **THERMOPYLAE**, would become a symbol of freedom for generations to come.

Herodotus writes about this battle:

"The havoc they caused to the enemy was tremendous. The Persian officers were thrashing and pushing the hoplites continuously forward, while the Hellenes mowed them down". "The battle was fierce. The Hellenes defended themselves to the last man. First they fought with the spears, then with the swords and in the end with tooth and nail. Leonidas fell amongst the first. Finally, they were all killed, because they were overwhelmed by the number of the enemy" (Herodotus Z' 229)

The Hellenic fleet, which until then had managed with tough resistance to stop the Persian fleet, learned of the events in Thermopylae, retreated through the Euboean Bay and arrived and was stationed at Salamis.

The Athenians abandoned their city and disembarked women and children at the Saronic islands and at Troezen.

At the same time Pythia was delivering oracles at Delphi saying that "Athens will be rescued by the wooden walls". Attica was swarmed by Xerxes' troops which arrive in Athens with no resistance to their advance, burning the temples and plundering works of art.

King Xerxes we have made it! Despite the difficulties, we are in Athens!

Send messengers to Susa to make known the joyful event and call the Pisistratides to take command of the city!

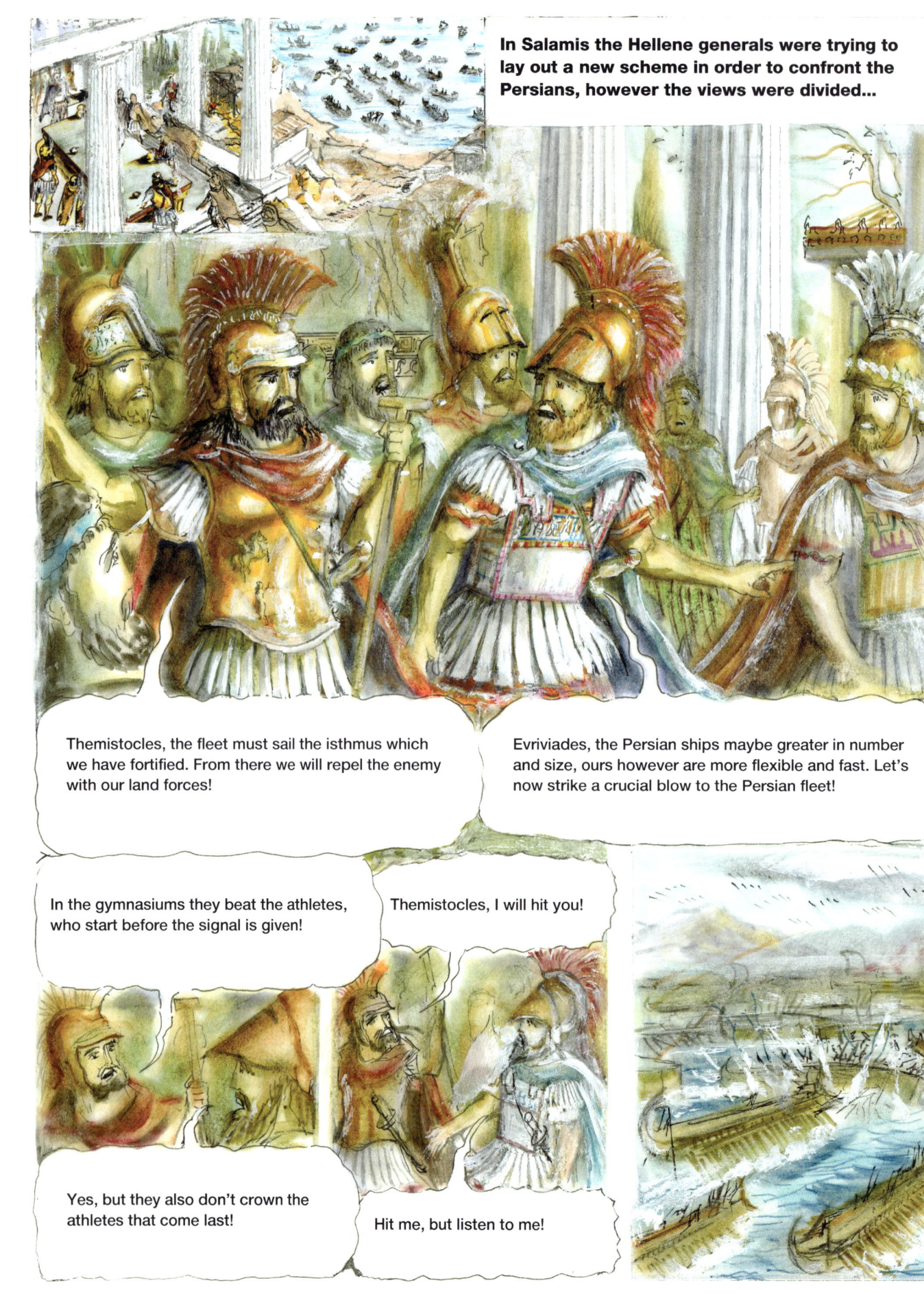

Evriviades was overpowered by Themistocles' admirable reply and heard his opinion. However he himself and the rest of the generals were not fully convinced. Themistocles retreated and resorted to a strategic ploy. He sent his loyal servant Sicinnus to Xerxes' headquarters with the purpose of misleading him. His message was that "The Hellenic fleet is intimidated and is preparing to leave Salamis. Tell him to hurry in order to block them and capture them."

Xerxes, who had already made the decision to attack the Hellenic fleet (he knew that the Hellenic ships were fewer) gave credence to Sicinnus' words.

At the crack of dawn from Aegina, Aristides saw the encircling movements of the Persian fleet. Without any delay he goes to Salamis where he narrates the events to the Generals' council. By now there is only one solution left....

In the morning 1200 Persian ships had been deployed facing 310 Hellenic.

The Hellenic trumpets sounded giving the signal for the outbreak of the naval battle. The Hellenic war-paean echoed in the blue horizon...

THE NAVAL BATTLE OF SALAMIS 480 B. C.
According to Themistocles' strategy the main attack of the Hellenes was mainly against the two outer ends of the Persian fleet. In this manner they were forcing them to retreat towards the center of the bay where they were clashing and suffering damages...

...the Hellene soldiers were unrivalled as they were free people willing to give their lives for the cause of freedom. After 12 hours, by sunset, the Persian fleet had been completely destroyed. The triumphant Hellenic fleet had been redeployed into battle positions.

Xerxes, with his staff offisers were watching the scenes of the fierce naval battle from mountain Egaleo...

The naval battle was titanic and lasted the whole day.
The Hellenic triremes were sinking the Persian ships with their rams, burning or capturing them in a hand-to-hand fight.
The Persians (together in their allies, Phoenicians and others) fought bravely. However the vehemence of the Hellenic ships and the spirit of...

Despot, we have suffered a harsh defeat. Nevertheless we have many and skilful infantrymen, nothing has yet been lost.

There is information that the Hellenic fleet could move quickly towards Hellespont and destroy the bridges! We should return...

However Mardonios, you who wanted this war so much, will stay in Hellas!

I leave you my best troops and you will carry on the hostilities after the end of the winter!

At the isthmus of Corinth, in Poseidon's temple, the united allies were gathered for the victory celebrations and in a festive atmosphere they rewarded all who excelled in the battles.

Mardonios, chose the convenient place where he would spend the winter and built a large camp to shelter his army.

DELPHI

We will take advantage of the winter. We will create favorable conditions till summer...

ATHENS

Mardonios encamped on the widest plain of Thessaly. His infantry together with his cavalry approached the 300.000 men.

Aristides, the Persian army still remains great. We have won the initial battles however, the final outcome of the war has not yet been determined.

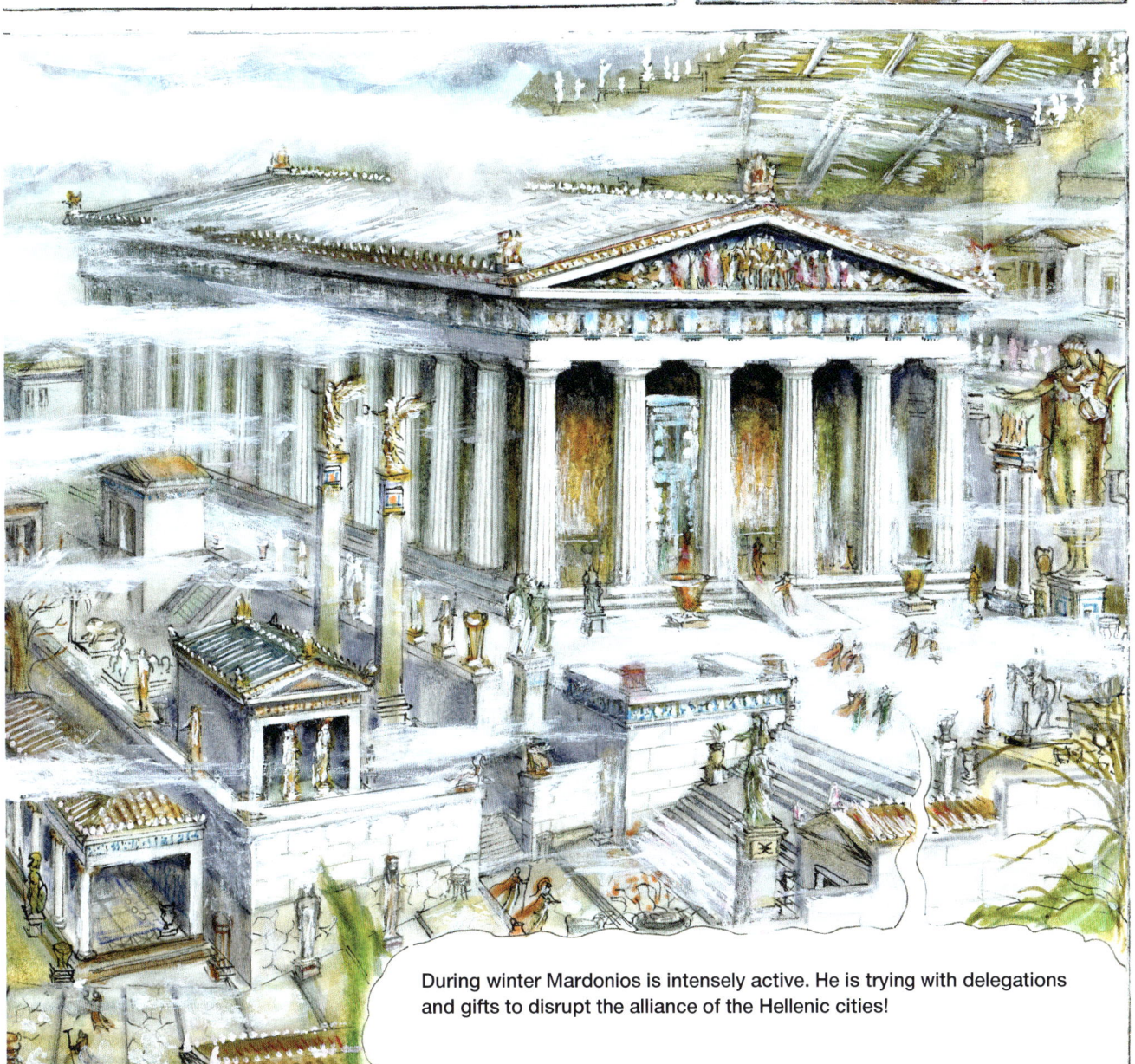

During winter Mardonios is intensely active. He is trying with delegations and gifts to disrupt the alliance of the Hellenic cities!

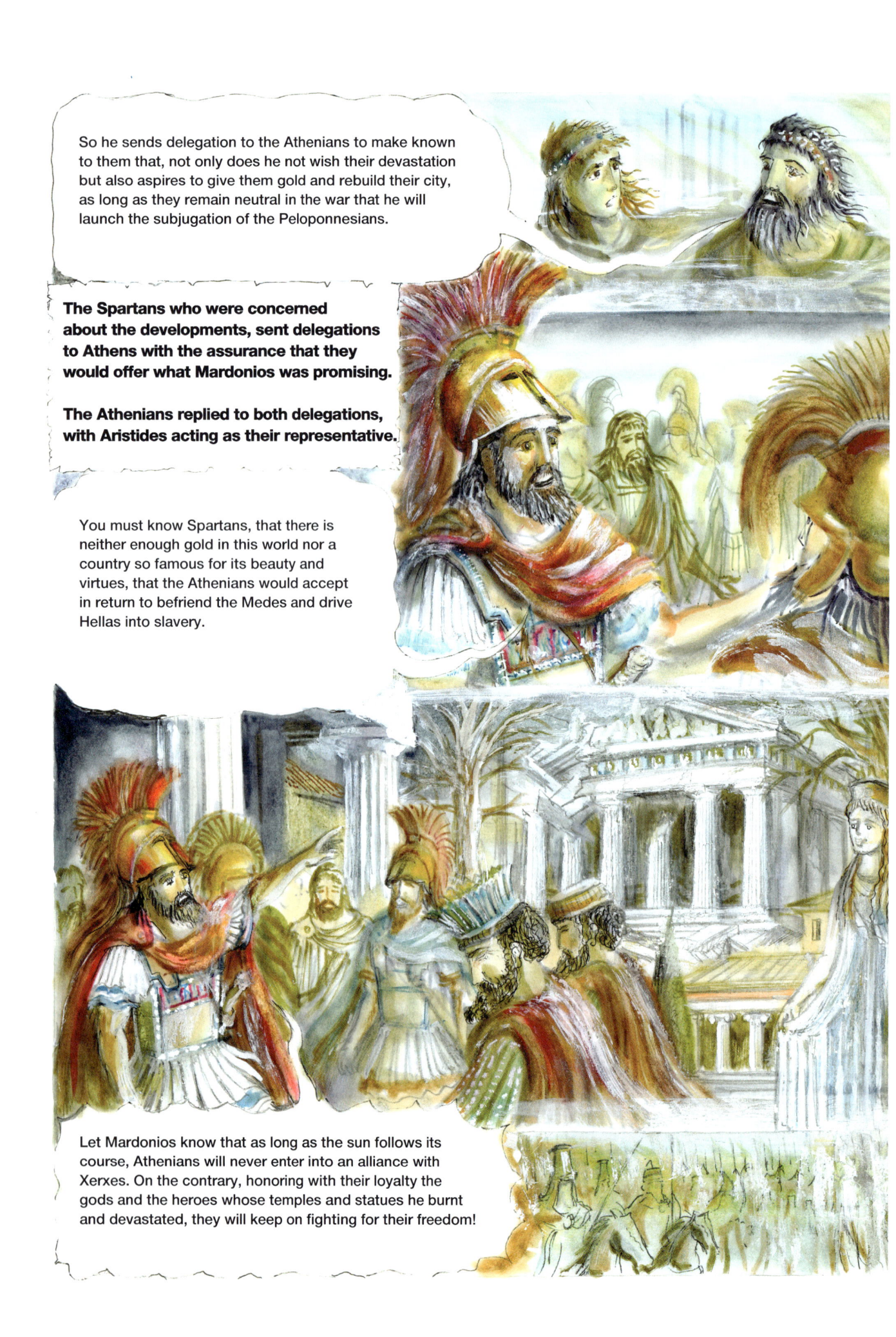

So he sends delegation to the Athenians to make known to them that, not only does he not wish their devastation but also aspires to give them gold and rebuild their city, as long as they remain neutral in the war that he will launch the subjugation of the Peloponnesians.

The Spartans who were concerned about the developments, sent delegations to Athens with the assurance that they would offer what Mardonios was promising.

The Athenians replied to both delegations, with Aristides acting as their representative.

You must know Spartans, that there is neither enough gold in this world nor a country so famous for its beauty and virtues, that the Athenians would accept in return to befriend the Medes and drive Hellas into slavery.

Let Mardonios know that as long as the sun follows its course, Athenians will never enter into an alliance with Xerxes. On the contrary, honoring with their loyalty the gods and the heroes whose temples and statues he burnt and devastated, they will keep on fighting for their freedom!

THE BATTLE OF PLATAEA
Spartans were filled with enthusiasm and joy upon hearing the responsible answer from the Athenians. On the contrary, Mardonios expressed his anger and rage, and set out with all his army, advanced into Athens in the summer of 479 B.C devastating all that had been left standing from the first raid (the Athenian women and children had left their city for the second time...)

Pausanias, Mardonios left Megara and is headed towards Plataea.

A very open setting, for the maneuvers of the persian cavalry. We will follow the Persian army.

At the same period the united Hellenic army had been amassed at isthmus and was heading towards Megara (100.000 hoplites with the Spartan Commander-in-Chief Pausanias), (while 8.000 were Athenians with Aristides as their general).

King Alexander, We were informed that the Persians are holding you as hostage!

Aristides, I managed to get away from the Persian guards. I am bringing valuable news!

PLATAEA

When Mardonios came to know of the movements of the Hellenic army, he retreated and encamped in Plataea.

Pausanias followed Mardonios to Plataea and encamped on the opposite hillocks. During the first 9 days the two enemies were avoiding to clash because in both encampments the omens had shown that the army which would put up a defense would win the battle.

Mardonios became aggravated by the wait and decided to attack on the 10th day...

Alexander the king of Macedonia, at night, made known to the Hellenic army Mardonios' decision. The great battle started the next morning. Its course developed in such a way that the most powerful strike by the Persians was delivered to the right side of the Hellenic front where the Spartan phalanx had lined up. The Hellenes pushed and drove the Persians away. The defeat of the Persian army was complete.

GREAT HELLAS
The burning of the Carthaginian fleet

> Our army has triumphed!
> All Hellas is celebrating!
> We are free! Every 5 years we will honor the anniversary of our victory in Plataea, with the festival "Eleftheria".

THE BATTLE OF MYCALE

On the same day the battle of Mycale took place. The united Hellenic fleet (110 ships) with their commanders the king of Sparta Leotychides and the Athenian general Xanthippus leave Delos, (after the call for assistance from the fraternal Ionian cities), arrive in Mycale where they set the Persian ships (300) on fire. The Hellene soldiers land and mount an attack which caused the Persian army to flee. After that, many Persian guards are forced out of the Persian coastline.

THE BATTLE OF HIMERA

As we have mentioned before, Carthage in 480 B.C went to war against the cities of Great Hellas.
Amilcas was at the head of the Carthaginians and his fleet was composed of 600 ships and 300.000 men. The leadership of the Hellenic forces was assumed by Gelon the tyrant of Syracuse together with Thiron from Agrigentum. In the intense battle that followed near the city Himera, the Carthaginians were defeated.

EPILOGUE OF THE PERSIAN WARS

After the outcome of the "Medians" the Hellenes honored the soldiers and generals, and especially Themistocles whose contribution was acknowledged by all the allies.
Alexander, king of Macedonia was pronounced a great personality amongst the Hellenes and his golden statue was set up in Delphi.
It took a lot of effort, pain, courage and hard work for the Hellenes to win their freedom as it is necessary for every human achievement.
The final outcome of the "Persian Wars" is regarded historic.
"Metropolitan Hellas" and the Europe avoided the Persian expansionism.

PROSPERITY AND HEGEMONY OF ATHENS

The period from 479 B.C till 431 B.C is called the "Fifty-year period" and is a period of prosperity and creativity for the Athenians. When Pausanias is accused by the Spartan trustees of holding consultations with the Persian court (an accusation later proven wrong), the allies then do not consent to the Spartan leadership and the Athenians grab the opportunity to take the lead of the Pan-Hellenic alliance (478 B.C).

Aristides fairly determines the contribution of men and money from each city to the alliance. Delos becomes the seat of the alliance.

In time the Athenian allied cities chose to offer money only, instead of ships and soldiers, gradually resulting in paying tribute to the Athenians. (In 425 B.C the alliance will add up to the maximum number of 400 cities).

During that period the Athenian fleet continues operations in the Aegean Sea with Aristides as their admiral and after 468 B.C with Kimon (Miltiades' son) they battled over and over again and totally pushed back the Persian fleet out of the Aegean Sea.

In 461 B.C the Athens-Sparta alliance was disrupted and from 460 B.C onwards one of the greatest figures in the Hellenic history appears, Pericles (son of Xanthippus and Agaristi).

DELOS

Kimon and the victories of the Eurymedon river (naval and land battle) was the last conflict after which the Persians started to withdraw from the Aegean sea.

The period that Pericles ruled Athens (till 429 B.C) is called symbolically by the historians "THE GOLDEN AGE OF PERICLES". The poets wrote about him when he was making a speech: "it was thundering and lightening and Hellas was shaken ..." He was righteously attributed the surname "Olympian" by the Athenians because he was solemn, noble and calm.

It was Pericles who took the initiative for the construction of the glorious monuments of Acropolis: Parthenon (with Ictinus and Callicrates as architects), the Propylaea, the Erechtheum with the Caryatids, the Pandrosio and others.)

During that period all social classes contributed to work and prosperity. It was characteristic that the slave who was a laborer at the time would get a higher wage than the free and specialized worker of the consequent ancient world. (The Hellenes like most people of the ancient world were using slaves, however their position in society was decent and protected by the law).

During the age of Pericles science, philosophy, theater and other human endeavors went through a period of intense development.

Athens became the intellectual and artistic center not only for Hellas but for the whole world! This was a status which Athens kept also during the Hellenistic and Roman period.

Aeschylus   Hippocrates   Aristophanes   Sofokles   Platon   Socrates

PELOPONNESIAN WAR
(431-404) B.C

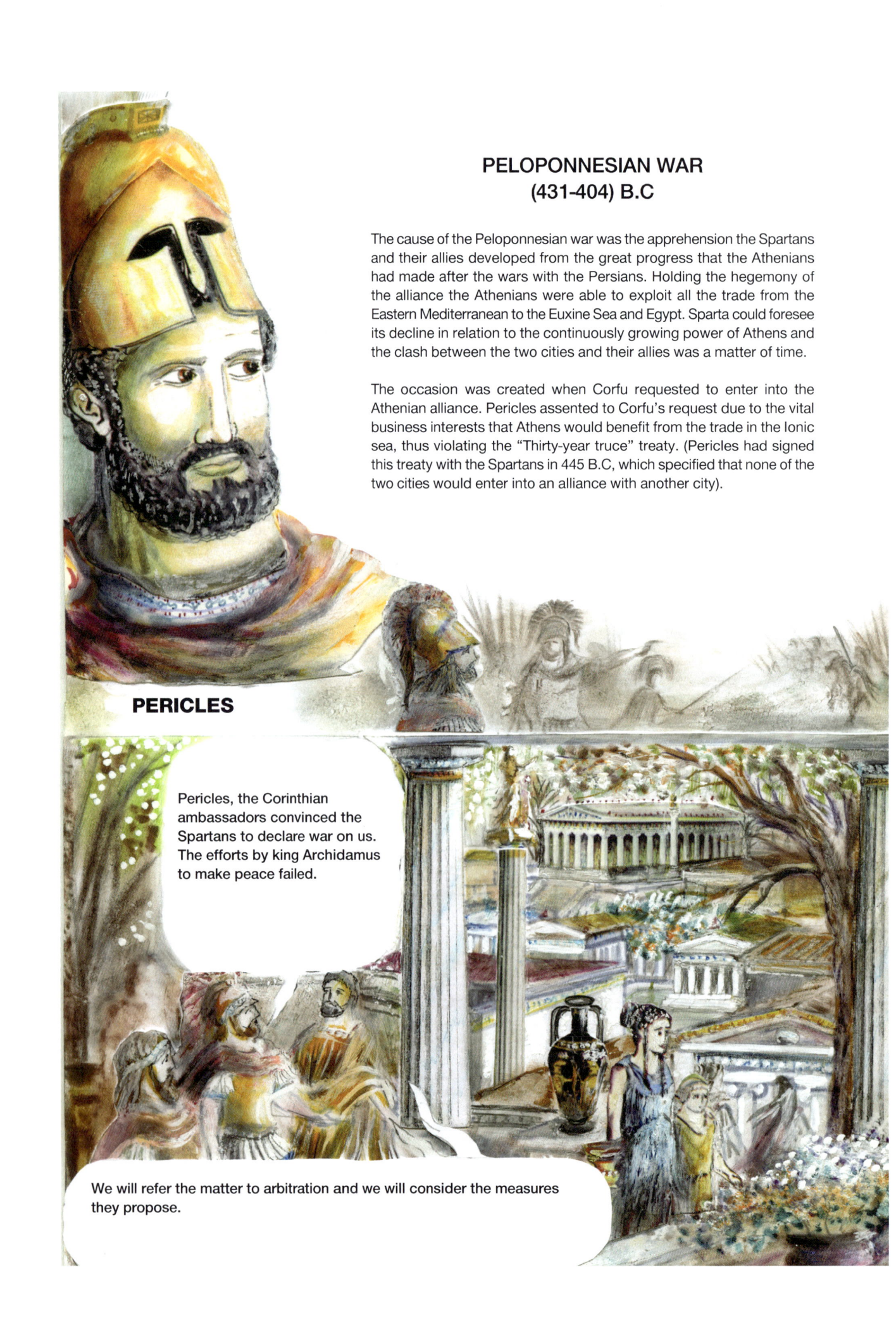

The cause of the Peloponnesian war was the apprehension the Spartans and their allies developed from the great progress that the Athenians had made after the wars with the Persians. Holding the hegemony of the alliance the Athenians were able to exploit all the trade from the Eastern Mediterranean to the Euxine Sea and Egypt. Sparta could foresee its decline in relation to the continuously growing power of Athens and the clash between the two cities and their allies was a matter of time.

The occasion was created when Corfu requested to enter into the Athenian alliance. Pericles assented to Corfu's request due to the vital business interests that Athens would benefit from the trade in the Ionic sea, thus violating the "Thirty-year truce" treaty. (Pericles had signed this treaty with the Spartans in 445 B.C, which specified that none of the two cities would enter into an alliance with another city).

PERICLES

Pericles, the Corinthian ambassadors convinced the Spartans to declare war on us. The efforts by king Archidamus to make peace failed.

We will refer the matter to arbitration and we will consider the measures they propose.

The 27 years are divided into 3 periods:
a) The decennial or Archidamus' war (431-421) B.C b) The peace period of Nikias (421-413) c) The Decelian and Ionian war (414-404). A crucial moment for the Athenians was when they blocked off 420 Spartans on the island of Sfaktiria (opposite Pylus), among them, hoplites from the most famous Spartan families. The Spartans were compelled to propose peace with the favorable pre-war conditions for Athens. However the Athenians, misled by Cleon, refused. In addition, since 403 the Athenian general Thrasivoulos, abolished the tyrannical regime of the "Thirty" which had been imposed by Sparta and restored democracy in Athens

The dispute was referred to arbitration, however the terms proposed by the Spartans were pointing to the elimination of the Athenian hegemony. As a result, the Athenians rejected the Spartans and war broke out. For 27 years the two sides (Athens and Sparta together with their allies) fought with each other. (The historian and general Thucydides recounted that period and its phases in a scientific way). Pericles' ingenious strategy consisted in defensive tactics on land (due to Athens' big walls and the strong Spartan infantry) and offensive in sea (the strength of the Athenian fleet was renowned). This strategy had positive results for Athens however Pericles' successors who were frivolous and driven by selfish motives abandoned it. (Like Cleon and Alciviades with the exception of Nikias who was a sensible general).

After a series of phases the decisive blow to Athens was given by the Spartan Lysander when he seized the Athenian fleet by a surprise attack at the "Egos potamous" (405 B.C) at the time the Athenians had disembarked.

The Spartans and their allies emerged as winners. When the Thebans and the Corinthians during the congress of the victors demanded to wipe out Athens from the face of the earth, Spartans showed prudence by replying: "It's not fair to devastate a Hellenic city which has offered valuable aid to Hellas against its greatest enemies."

NIKIAS

During the period of Spartan hegemony approximately 13.000 Hellene soldiers arrived in Persia to support Satrap Cyrus, who was claiming the Persian throne. After Cyrus' death they were forced to return on their own. They survived an epic march of extreme hardships and attacks. It was the famous "The descent of the ten thousand" which was written by Xenophon (a general which was chosen by the hoplites, for their return) (401).

After an appeal which was launched by the Ionian cities (400-399) the Spartans rallied to their support and at river Paktolos (395) the Spartan Agesilaus (with 8.000 men) defeated the Persians and conceived the plan for the disruption of the Persian state. At that time the Persian general Tithraustes sent plentiful money to Hellas and formed an anti-Spartan alliance (from Thebans, Corinthians, Argies, Athenians) and as a result Agesilaus is called back to Sparta.

LYSANDER

The only sovereign power that was left was Sparta. They started to oppress the Hellenic cities, to set up oligarchic regimes and impose higher taxes than those previously taken by the Athenians. This period is known as the HEGEMONY OF SPARTA (404-371) B.C.. The Spartan allies were displeased as they didn't benefit from the treaties and an anti-Spartan alliance started to form by the Thebans and the Corinthians which eventually led to clashes with Sparta.

The Thebans took advantage of this period of attrition and formed a powerful army with the efficient generals Pelopidas and Epaminondas. Its elite force was the Holly Legion and a new military tactic was employed, the "Oblique phalanx".
Sparta clashes with Thebes. In the battle of Leuctra (371) the Thebans win (for the first time in 500 years, an army with Spartan soldiers in its ranks is defeated). The HEGEMONY OF THEBES begins.

Thebes' power grows rapidly as Hellenic cities and kingdoms enter into their alliance. Athens and Sparta, former opponents, now ally against Thebes....

The battle in Mantinea (362 B.C) between the Thebans and the alliance of Spartans, Athenians, Arcadians and others signified the end of Thebes' hegemony although they were able to prevail. The gradual loss of Thebes' efficient generals also helped to bring about this downfall.

By now no Hellenic city or kingdom has the power to have control over Hellas. Xenophon writes: "Now there is even greater confusion and unrest in Hellas, than there was before the battle".

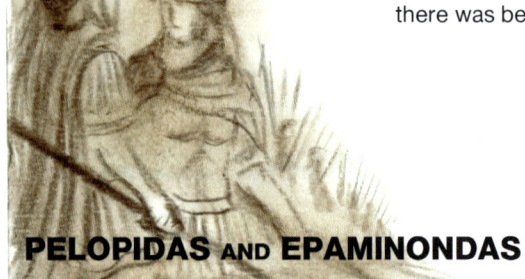

PELOPIDAS AND EPAMINONDAS

THE PRIME OF MACEDONIA AND PHILIP B'

The successive civil wars created a state of disorganization and distress in the Hellenic area. At that critical moment in the history of the Hellenic nation Macedonia emerges, full of energy and strength. The Macedonians had kept the primitive regime of the Homeric monarchy in which the king was governing together with the aristocrats and the big land-owners who were called "Eteri" (Associates).

Initially the inhabitants were farmers and stock-breeders, while during the 6th century B.C they develop their own trade and small industries. King Archelaus A' (413-399) transfers the capital of Macedonia from Aigai (Edessa) to Pella where he built marvelous palaces which gradually covered an area of 60.000 square meters.

Philip B' was born in 382 B.C in Pella. He was the son of king Amyntas IB' and Eurydice.

In 350 B.C he assumed the reins of monarchy in Macedonia and devoted himself to the organization of his army and kingdom.

Philip invented an unprecedented innovation for the infantry, the Macedonian phalanx with 4.000 hoplites. The men were arrayed in 16 lines and each one was armed with a very long spear of 6,30 meters length (sarisses) forming a moving fortress of spearheads. The flanks of the phalanx were protected by light-armed hoplites and the spear throwers and archers followed. They were supported by additional infantry troops (select foot guards) and the Macedonian cavalry (comrades- "eteri"). With his highly trained army he was able to save his country from the raids of the Illyrians and Thracians and puts his plan into further practice. In 357 B.C at the age of 25 he marries Olympiada, an orphan princess of Epirus from the royal house of Eacides.

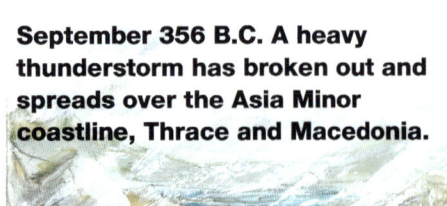

September 356 B.C. A heavy thunderstorm has broken out and spreads over the Asia Minor coastline, Thrace and Macedonia.

THE PALACES OF PELLA
Philip returned pleased to Pella after having conquered the gold-bearing region of Paggeo. His joy is even greater for his new-born son Alexander. The next 3 years Macedonia's economy thrives under Philip's leadership. (He builds ships, gains mastery over Potidea and the influential Methoni). However in 353 B.C the Holly war breaks out in Hellas...

PELLA

Our queen has given birth! Aeropos! Olympiada has given birth...

Hellanices, Philip is situated in the Paggeo region. I will send a messenger to inform him.

EPHESUS

Somewhere at this very moment a torch was lit up, a flame was born, which some day will set fire to the Eastern world.

Artemis' temple is on fire!

I know my friends, that the complaints from the Thebans that the Phoceans encroached and cultivated areas that belonged to the oracle at Delphi are true. In addition the Phoceans formed an allience with the Pherreans...

King Philip! They have formed an army of over 20.000 men! We the Aleuades who reign over Larisa will fight for the hegemony of all the people in Thessaly. We are asking for your help to strike the sacrilegious.

It was an additional challenge for the clever king to get involved in the issues of southern Hellas, as his plan was to unite the Hellenes.

Philip went to Thessaly but the Phocean general Enomarchus beats him in two consecutive battles. Philip did not give up and in the spring of 352 B.C leads his army to Thessaly where he beats his opponents in the battle that followed.

The Thessalians greeted him as their liberator and savior also the renowned Thessalian cavalry from now on will follow the fearless Macedonian kings everywhere.

I accept your call! We will defend the age-old Hellenic traditions and we will push back the trespassers.

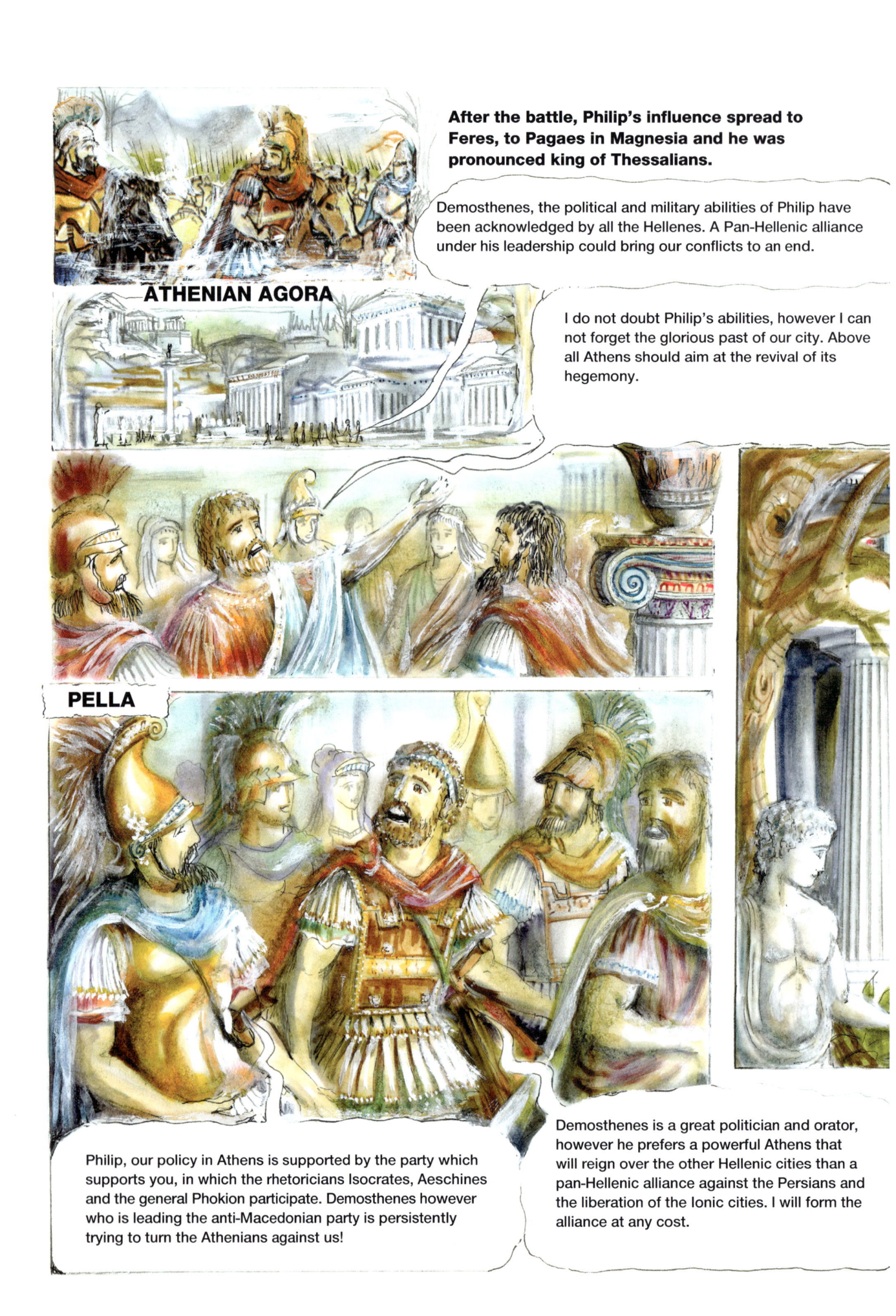

After the battle, Philip's influence spread to Feres, to Pagaes in Magnesia and he was pronounced king of Thessalians.

Demosthenes, the political and military abilities of Philip have been acknowledged by all the Hellenes. A Pan-Hellenic alliance under his leadership could bring our conflicts to an end.

ATHENIAN AGORA

I do not doubt Philip's abilities, however I can not forget the glorious past of our city. Above all Athens should aim at the revival of its hegemony.

PELLA

Philip, our policy in Athens is supported by the party which supports you, in which the rhetoricians Isocrates, Aeschines and the general Phokion participate. Demosthenes however who is leading the anti-Macedonian party is persistently trying to turn the Athenians against us!

Demosthenes is a great politician and orator, however he prefers a powerful Athens that will reign over the other Hellenic cities than a pan-Hellenic alliance against the Persians and the liberation of the Ionic cities. I will form the alliance at any cost.

After the Hellenic-Persian wars, the Persian royal court changed its policy and the way they were dealing with the Hellenic issues. The Persians realized that conflicting interests developed amongst us and started to support various sides with a great deal of gold and with the purpose of boosting our conflicts while aiming at a war of attrition. We are all responsible, nevertheless the Persians will remain our great threat as long as we are not united.

During the same period there was tension between the Hellenes in "Great Hellas" and the Carthaginians and a new conflict wouldn't be far off. SYRACUSE...

During the recent conflicts the Carthaginians in collaboration with brotherly Hellenic cities seized Selinus, Thermes and Heraclea Minoa.

Our city has weakened and it won't take long for the Carthaginians to attack! Let's send a messenger to our metropolis Corinth, for reinforcements.

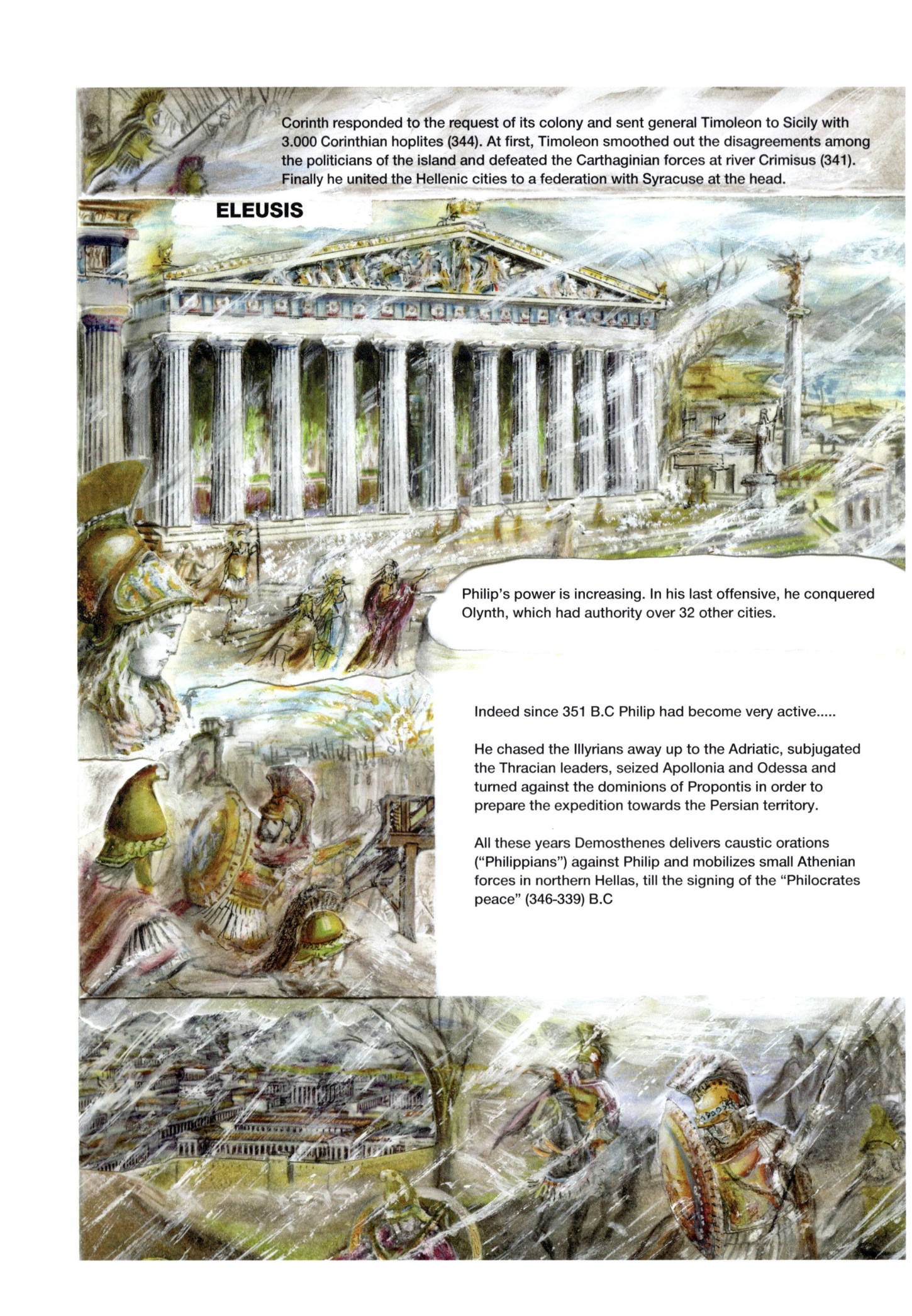

Corinth responded to the request of its colony and sent general Timoleon to Sicily with 3.000 Corinthian hoplites (344). At first, Timoleon smoothed out the disagreements among the politicians of the island and defeated the Carthaginian forces at river Crimisus (341). Finally he united the Hellenic cities to a federation with Syracuse at the head.

ELEUSIS

Philip's power is increasing. In his last offensive, he conquered Olynth, which had authority over 32 other cities.

Indeed since 351 B.C Philip had become very active.....

He chased the Illyrians away up to the Adriatic, subjugated the Thracian leaders, seized Apollonia and Odessa and turned against the dominions of Propontis in order to prepare the expedition towards the Persian territory.

All these years Demosthenes delivers caustic orations ("Philippians") against Philip and mobilizes small Athenian forces in northern Hellas, till the signing of the "Philocrates peace" (346-339) B.C

CHERONEA

Their forces add up to approximately 30.000 hoplites.

Alexander my son, their strength is equal to ours.

In order to safeguard his Northeastern borders, Philip marches out against the Skythian king Atea, while his 17 year old son Alexander, against the Medarians. Father and son return victoriously to Pella (339). The people sing victorious hymns and insist to see Philip who is hesitant due to an injury...

Alexander is holding him saying:

"Courage, father! March proudly. Every step of yours is a reminder of the struggle towards virtue!"

In the spring of 338 Philip makes his way down to Phokis (after an invitation from the Amphictyonic conference).

At Demosthenes' instigation, Thebes and Athens send an army against him. Philip asks for peaceful negotiations yet his proposal is turned down. During the wavering battle which took place in the plain of Cheronea (338 B.C) Philip prevailed.

The next day when some suggested to Philip to destroy Athens, he replied: "I went through all these tortures and dangers in order to win glory and you now want me to destroy the heart of this glory?

The Gods wouldn't want this!"

Thus he negotiated the peace terms with prudence and equity, gaining everybody's recognition and admiration.

In 337 B.C he convenes a meeting in Corinth with representatives from all the Hellenic cities (except Sparta) and is unanimously proclaimed Commander-in-Chief of Hellas. There he also develops the military plans against the Persians.
Before the winter sets in Philip is making war preparations without asking for support from the allied cities. The remaining Hellenic expeditionary forces would then also come to Pella.

In September 336 in the old capital Aigai the great king was celebrating his daughter's wedding together with other festivities. The moment the crowd had burst into greeting cheers: "LONG LIVE THE KING.....LONG LIVE THE KING!" he is assassinated.

As it was written by his uncompromised adversary Demosthenes, Philip was: "THE GREATEST AND MOST SKILFUL OF ALL THE QUOTED PERSONS IN ALL AGES."

ALEXANDER THE GREAT AND THE SPREADING OF THE HELLENIC CIVILIZATION

Alexander was just 20 years old when he was proclaimed king of Macedonia by the army in September of 336 B.C.

Since he was a child his teachers, Lysimachus from Acarnania and Leonidas, taught him moderation, self-restraint and self-control.

Philip later brought Aristotle to Pella who taught him sciences and philosophy.

At the age of 12 Alexander breaks in the wild Thessalian horse Bucephalus which will become his partner in all his later expeditions. At that moment, Philip embraces him with eyes filled with tears of joy and says to him: "My son, make sure that you find another kingdom as Macedonia is too small for you!"

OLYMPIA

Actions are stronger than words. Alexander's rapid movements managed to control the Pan-Hellenic alliance and earn the admiration of all.

Indeed, he went down to Thessaly with his army and after avoiding the Thessalian army which was situated in Tempi, he marched in an easterly direction to Peneus' mouth and climbed up the woody and inaccessible Ossa, bypassed Pagasitikos...

....so he arrived at Fthiotida and Thebes. He puzzled the Thessalians with his achievement to escape notice and cut them off from their mountains.

The reconciliation of the Hellenes which was attained by Philip's efforts was now in danger due to the withdrawal of some cities.

PELLA

That is why they hastened to return into the alliance. The representatives of the other cities in Thebes also did the same. Alexander overlooked their disobedience. In Delphi's Amphictyony and in the Pan-Hellenic conference in Corinth he was proclaimed General of the Army of all the Hellenes.

The corps of engineers, the medical corps and the topographical service should be organized. All must be considered wisely for the expedition against the Persians.

Alexander, in the spring they will be ready. However when we advance into Asia, our northern boundaries will be exposed to the raids of the northern tribes.

In that case, general Antipatros will remain in Pella with 12.000 infantrymen and 1.500 horsemen. As a precaution in order to push them back we will march out against them.

In the spring of 335 B.C Alexander crossed the valley of Nestos and Evros and arrived at the gate of Misia, where at a pass of the mountain Haemus he fought the first victorious battles with the local tribes, at an altitude of 2.500 meters.

Then he advanced further northwards (500 kms) up to Danube....

...He fought and pushed back the Triballi, while the Gets and Celts declared their amity. During his return he is informed that the Illyrians with the Tavlantians are heading for war against Macedonia. Without further delay he hastened to come up against them and defeats them at Lake Lychnitis. He then chased them up to their inaccessible mountains. Then news comes from central Hellas...

If Demosthenes considers me a "child" here in the northern mountains, then I will stand as a teenager before the walls of Thebes and a man in front of Athens!

King Alexander, there is a rumor going around that you have been mortally wounded. The Thebans withdrew from the alliance, while Charidimus and Demosthenes who characterizes you as "child" are urging the Athenians to do the same!

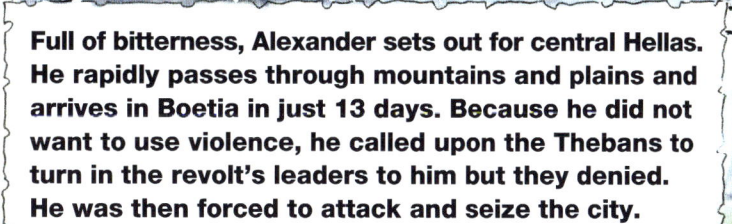

Full of bitterness, Alexander sets out for central Hellas. He rapidly passes through mountains and plains and arrives in Boetia in just 13 days. Because he did not want to use violence, he called upon the Thebans to turn in the revolt's leaders to him but they denied. He was then forced to attack and seize the city.

Alexander, if you want to prevent social upheavals in Hellas, you make peace urgently. If again you want glory, use your army against the foreigners!

Phokion, I want peace for all our brothers and alliance for the common cause. The only thing I ask is for Charidimos to be exiled as he is the one who roused Athens.

ACROPOLIS OF ATHENS

Phokion, after the Persian wars, a lot of us envisaged a Pan-Hellenic union, yet it was Philip who accomplished it. Alexander continues this dream.

In October at Isthmus the representatives of the Hellenic cities with Alexander at the head held a meeting for the expeditionary plans and the forces that each city would contribute.

The total force consisted of 30.000 infantrymen and 5.000 horsemen with the Macedonian phalanx (12.000), the foot-guards, the Macedonian cavalry (1.500 comrades and 500 scouts), the heavy Thessalian cavalry (1.500), Acarnanian and Aetolian infantry (5.000), 7.000 soldiers and 600 horsemen from the other allied cities, 160 ships (many of them Athenian) and 500 renowned Cretan archers.

Alexander, the remaining Hellenic forces will be concentrated on Pella during spring...

SUSA

I am unable to comprehend how a young Hellene king with a small in number army is threatening our empire.

In Autumn we will all gather at Isthmus in order to organize the expedition against the Persians and the liberation of their subject people.

Darius my Great Master, the Hellenic army is small and yet organized in an excellent way. Memnon recommends we ravage the areas and close in upon Alexander in the vastness of the country.

We do not need actions like these! Send word to my officers that if the audacious youngster passes Hellespont, they should capture him, flog him and make him an example and send him as a prisoner to Susa!

During spring 334 B.C Alexander sets out for the big venture. The Hellenes would confront the large and well armed Persian army commanded by Darius III the Codomanus.

Alexander, you have portioned out all the royal land and income to your comrades! What have you kept for yourself?

Alexander led his army to Sestos of Hellespont where with the fleet's assistance they landed in Asia near ancient Troy. In Arisvi he was informed that the Persians were waiting for him at the Granic river and he hastened to confront them....

My hopes!

The Persian army is situated in an advantageous position behind the river and has approximately 20.000 horsemen and even more infantrymen. I recommend that we encamp today and attack tomorrow.

Parmenion, I am aware of all that you are telling me, yet if I have second thoughts in every creek that I meet I will only boost the Persians' morale.

Alexander gave the signal for the attack and the first division of troops rushed at the Granic river shouting the ancient Hellenic battle cry "Enyalios!" However they were greeted by a shower of spears and arrows.

The trumpets blared forth and the remaining cavalry with Alexander at its head moved as a body with such a strong momentum that they penetrated deeply into the Persian disposition and with severe battles pushed back the Persians.

Officers and hoplites be brave!

As soon as Parmenion with the phalanxes came to the opposite bank, the Persians panicked and fled. After the battle, Alexander passed down the ranks and gave courage to the wounded.

Alexander has not yet seen the real strength of my Empire. I am preparing an army of 500.000 infantrymen and 100.000 horsemen!

Despot, after our defeat, Alexander proceeds to the liberation of the coastal Hellenic cities. Memnon has fortified and guards only Miletus and Alikarnassos with 400 ships and 80.000 men.

Indeed, Alexander arrives in Sardinia where he is greeted as their honorable liberator and afterwards he frees Smyrna and Ephesus where the people cheer him enthusiastically.

After hard sieges he frees Miletus and Alikarnassos. Then he forces the Persians out from the mountainous places of Pamphylia and Pisidia and arrives at the Gordian where he unties the renowned Gordian knot (it is likely that he cut it with his sword).

MILETUS

In May of 333 B.C (having covered more than 2.800 kms from Pella) he marches out northeast subjugating Cappadocia and Cilicia and frees Tarsus an old Ionic colony.

In October of the same year he is informed of the movements of Darius' strong army and hurries off to come up against it. He advances through the autumn rains and windstorms and arrives at Isso's plain where Darius had encamped.

Alexander, we have been informed that Darius is mustering a great army!

We will come up against Darius' army however we won't change our initial plan for the liberation of the coastline region down to Egypt.

THE BATTLE IN ISSO (November 333 B.C)

Alexander spoke with self-confidence to the generals and soldiers and imparted his enthusiasm to the troops...

The battle was powerful. The Hellenic center puts up a strong defense and keeps in check the confronting Persians.

The phalanxes on the left flank (commanded by Parmenion) struggle to bear all the brunt of the attack of the Persian cavalry...

Alexander leads the cavalry on the right side defying the rain of spears and arrows, breaking through the enemy lines.

...He approaches Darius' chariot and a fierce battle follows during which Darius is put to flight together with large parts of his army.

Alexander, amongst the prisoners is Darius' royal family as well as many Persian noblewomen.

Offer them all the respect and goods they have had in their lives up to this day. Also, attend to all the wounded.

The next day Alexander looked on, on all the wounded although he himself was seriously injured. Afterwards he marched out along the Phoenician coastline. The cities Bible and Sidon surrendered to him yet Tyre which is an ally of the Persians stood out against him...

"Tyre is built with powerful walls on a rugged and impregnable island. Its siege is almost impossible!"

"Nothing is impossible! We will make dike from the seashore up to the island for the siege machines and at the same time we will blockade them with the fleet."

After 7 months of hard siege Tyre was taken (July 332). In terms of effort and energy no other siege in world history could be compared to it. (According to E. Schramm).

During that period Darius was preparing an army considerably larger than the one he had disposed in Isso...

Alexander arrived in Ilioupolis and afterwards with a full naval and army force he crossed the Nile and entered triumphantly in Memphis of Egypt....

The Persian satraps surrendered themselves and the people of Egypt received him with inexpressible joy as their liberator and a person who carries on the Pharaoh's traditions.

They named him prince of victory, lord of the two countries, the chosen one of the king-Sun and many more...

Alexander organized parades and festivals meanwhile assigning the religious and civil government to the Egyptians and the military and economic planning to the Hellenes...

In April of 331 B.C he set out to the depths of Asia. An unimaginable world opened before the Hellenes by the vastness of the lands and the sharp fluctuations of the weather conditions.

Alexander crosses Syria and the river Euphrates. He covers 450 kms up to North Mesopotamia and with difficulty crosses the river Tiger.

Alexander arrived 10 kms away from Gavgamila, the plain on where Darius had encamped with an army consisting of 1.000.000 infantrymen, 40.000 cavalry, chariots and elephants. On the other hand the Hellenes were 40.000 infantrymen and 7.000 horsemen.

Alexander, the Persians are double in size and well organized, compared to Isso. I recommend we should take them by surprise with a night attack.

I want an up-front victory!

THE BATTLE IN GAVGAMILA (OCTOBER 331 B.C)

The next morning, Alexander on Bucephalus was heartening the hoplites and gave signal for the outbreak of the battle.

The battle was fearsome and lasted the whole day….Chariots, horsemen, hoplites, overturned. Alexander was twice encircled by countless Persian cavalry and infantry. The phalanxes commanded by Parmenion are broken by strong forces of Persian and Indian cavalry…

Alexander wins the battle thanks to his decisive attack on the Persian center where Darius is situated and drives him to flight. He then returns to help the remaining army thus resulting to the Persian's general retreat.

After the great Hellenic victory the Persian Empire was disrupted. Alexander makes his way towards Babylon where its big gates opened and he was received by the people as their saver.

End of November he arrives in Susa (renowned for its immense wealth). He settled Darius' family in the winter royal palace and organized festivals and torchlight processions spreading the news that a new era of freedom and progress is dawning.

The following years Alexander sets out for new expeditions. He advances southeast and enters into Persepolis (religious center) and into Ecvatana (Median capital, 330 B.C), crosses Zadracarta and Arachosia. From 329 till 327 he passes the snowy Indian Caucasus (from passages at 3.500 meters altitude) and crosses Bactriana and Sogdiani of the 1.000 cities under extremely difficult conditions.

In April of 327 he crosses the Indus river plain (Indian campaign) where local leaders make their submission to him. In 326 he arrives at Hydaspes river and at the opposite bank the intrepid king Porus of Pentapotamia had disposed 50.000 infantrymen, 4.000 horsemen and 300 tower-bearing elephants.

During the fierce battle that followed Alexander prevailed and treated Porus with generosity. By now the snow white peaks of the Himalayas opened out in the horizon and Alexander wished to keep on marching forward. However, his comrades-in-arms refused, exhausted by this inconceivable titanic march from the Aegean Sea to the Indian Ocean.

Thus in September of 326 he took the road back, crossing the dry desert of Gedrosia (under horrid conditions) and in 324 came to Pasargades and afterwards to Susa where he organized festivals and games.

Along this route, he built numerous cities in the places where he passed. In Babylon he was received by delegations with presents from all over the world as the one and only master of the planet. Motivated by his tireless and unsubdued nature he was making new plans for expeditions to the West. However in 323 at the age of 33 years he falls gravely ill.

On the last day of his life he makes his farewells to all his comrades-in-arms who pass sorrowfully before him.

Alexander left civilizing and cosmogonic work, spread the anthropocentric Hellenic civilization to the known world of his era and gave freedom and respect to the people of his Empire. Most historians agree that nobody else was worthy enough of the title "Great".

ACROPOLIS OF PERGAMUS

EMPIRE OF ALEXANDER THE GREAT

HELLENISTIC PERIOD
(323-167) B.C

The vast empire was divided into large provinces under the command of the generals of Alexander the Great. It was decided that Alexander's step brother, Philip Arrideos, together with Roxanne's child, (the pregnant wife of Alexander the Great), should jointly reign over the whole dominion.

With the passing of time the descendants of the Hellene generals formed states which were called Hellenistic (because their character and civilization were profoundly Hellenic). Those were: a) The Egyptian or Ptolemaic state (The richest and most powerful with its capital Alexandria) b) the state of Seleucides (the largest in area with Seleucia as its capital and afterwards the famous Antioch which for 1000 years was the metropolis of Hellenes) c) the kingdom of Pergamus, also known as New Hellas.

In Metropolitan Hellas except for the Macedonian kingdom and the city-states other significant powers had also emerged like the state of Epirus (composed of the Hellenic tribes of Molossians, Thesprotes, Chaones and others) known also by king Pyrrhus, the Aetolian confederacy with Thermo as its center and the Achaicus confederacy with Aegio as its center.

The Hellenistic capitals were radiant with the cultivation of arts and letters and traded from the Mediterranean down to India and China.

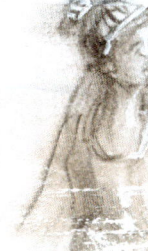

PTOLEMY

ANTIOCHUS

SELEUCUS

EUMENES

CLEOPATRA **HYPATIA**  **EUKLID** **ARCHIMEDES**  **PYRRHUS**

FOOTNOTES

Page 13: The Spartans had kept the uncommon constitution of double monarchy (In that period Leonidas and Evriviades jointly reigned). Higher political members were the Senate (2 kings and 28 elder statesmen) and the Ephors, who in the course of time attained power and controlled the kings.

Page 14: Priene which is shown in the icon is the city that started being built after 450 B.C. The old Priene had been built in the 11th century B.C 15 kms further away, along the banks of the river Meander.

Page 15: The temple of Artemis in Corfu (in the early 6th century) is one of the earlier temples of Dorian order with 8 pillars in its width (17 in its length) and it was one of the finest pieces of work of the archaic era.

Page 17: At the suggestion of Ippias, the Persians disembarked at Marathon as a part of the area's population had sympathetic feelings towards him. Ippias was an exile tyrant of Athens in the Persian court (son of Pisistratus).

Page 18: As the Persian fleet was leaving, it didn't turn towards Asia but towards Sounio, in the direction of Phaleron (They thought that they will find Athens unguarded). Miltiades left Aristides in Marathon to watch over the looting. He left with the remaining troops and deployed them in Cynosarges...
In the morning when the Persians saw the Athenian armor shining under the sun got discouraged and changed tack.

Page 20: 20 years after Solon's legislation 3 political parties had been formed in Athens: a) The party of "Pedieon", (all the aristocracy), b) The party of "Paraliakon", (traders, mariners, craftsmen) c) The party of "Diakrion", (stock-breeders and farmers).

Page21: At that period Macedonia is a Hellenic kingdom, of limited financial and military power, not yet having the great strength it will acquire 130 years later.

Page 22: The most significant administrative and religious centers of Persia were Susa and Persepolis. The royal center which appears in the icon had started being built after 490 B.C and Ionian masters participated in its construction.

Page 23: Corinth was one of the strong city-states of the era with intense trading activity and foundation of great colonies (like Syracuse, Corfu and others). It's agora with Apollo's temple is shown in the icon (with the exceptional monolithic pillars), public buildings and arcades.

Page 24: 3 temples stand on the opposite hill of Selinounta. The segment which is visible was one of the greatest temples (of Dorian order) that existed. The height of the pillars reached 16.5 meters.

Page 25: The temple of Artemis in Ephesus (Artemisio) was a superb architectural conception of Ionian order. (Beginning of construction 560 B.C), (Dimensions: 115.14 m x 55.10 m) (side pillars 8 X 21). The height of the pillars approached to 18.90 m and they were 106 in total.
The architects were the son of Metagenis from Knossos, Chersifronas and Theodoros of Roikos who had designed the temple of Hera in Samos.

Page 26: Sparta was famous for the austere and hard training of its soldiers. It was built in a gifted natural environment between the mountains Taygetus and Parnon and the river Eurotas. The Spartans were also called Lacedaemonians by the first king of Sparta Lacedaemon.
It was a great honor for the Spartans to defend their country and made famous the expression which the Spartan women used when sending their sons off to battle and giving them the shield: "Either with it or on it".

Page 34: The right flank of the Hellenic disposition was occupied by the naval squadrons of Sparta, Corinth, Aegina and Megara, the Athenian ships on the left and the ships of the smaller cities in the center. (The triremes had 3 rows of 30 oarsmen on each side, 280 in total).

Page 37: Delphi was built amphitheatrically in a landscape of unrivaled natural beauty on Parnassus' mountainside at an approximately 550 meters altitude where the lively waters of fountain Castalia spring up. It was one of the most important (among hundreds of sacred grounds) spiritual and religious Hellenic centers. It was regarded as the center of the earth (navel of the earth).
In the icon one can discern the theater, the temple of Apollo, the colossal statue of Apollo Sitalia. During the Hellenistic period Delphi was adorned with similar buildings.

Page 44: In the icon Acropolis is shown as well as a section of the Athenian agora as it was during the Roman era. In comparison to the golden age of Pericles where Acropolis is identical, in the agora there are also the two-storey arcade of Attalos, Agrippa's conservatory and the temple of Mars.

Page 50: The construction for the new Artemisio will commence a few years later, during the liberation of Ephesus, when Alexander the Great gave order for the erection of a new temple funded by the tax that the Ephessians were paying to the Persians. The new temple was a masterpiece and was one of the 7 wonders of the ancient world.
The other wonders of the ancient world were: The pyramids of Egypt, the hanging garden of Babylon, the statue of gold and ivory of Zeus (in Olympia), the mausoleum of Alikarnassus, the Colossus of Rhodes (it stood up in the harbor and exceeded the 30 meters height) and the lighthouse of Alexandria (135 meters height).

Page 51: The Macedonians regarded Hercules as their first ancestor. According to tradition, 3 royal princes (the Timenides), Gavanis, Aeropos and Perdiccas set out before 700 B.C from Argos of Peloponnese and arrived at the scenic Edessa where they established the Macedonian Kingdom.

Page 54: The Hellenic states were autonomus (city-states). This inevitably led to disputes and conflicts among them (There were also councils the "Amphictyonies" in which peaceful settlements of disputes were sought after). Under those conditions it was difficult for Phillip to peacefully band all of them together into one nation with common objectives. For this reason, he had to strengthen his Kingdom and if needed to gain control over the others.

Page 56: The Olympic Games took place every 4 years in the sacred place of Olympia (the first were organized in 776 B.C). The Philipium, (the dome of Ionian order in honor of Philip B') is shown in the icon behind it is the temple of Hera, on the right the great temple of Zeus and in the distance the arcade of Echo. In the area there were also other sanctuaries, guest rooms, big buildings, parliament, prytaneum, theater, stadion treasures and others.
The Zeu's statue of gold and ivory (13.50 meters height) was made by Pheidias.

Page 60: All the states participated in the Pan-Hellenic Congress in Corinth aside from Sparta which responded egotistically, saying that they are usually the leaders and not the followers. The Persians and Darius knew the expeditionary plans of Alexander and were trying to stop him.
Thus the Persian agents in Hellas having as an argument the autonomy of the states and the plentiful Persian gold they were trying to sway politicians and generals and disrupt the Pan-Hellenic alliance.
The highest command of the infantry was entrusted to the experienced Parmenion, the navy to the Cretan Nearchos, the corps of engineers to Diades, and the cavalry to the son of general Filotas. There were also other generals like Dimaratos, Lysimachos, Lennatos, Nicanoras, Antigonos, Meleagros, Perdicas and others.

Page 61: Parthenon is the crowning creation of the ancient Hellenic architecture (in relation to the temples of Dorian order). The temple gives the illusion that it is composed of straight lines, while in fact it is made up of gentle curves! (Length, width, gables, pillars which slightly tilt inwards and others).

Pages 62, 63, 64: Alexander paid a visit to ancient Troy in the Asia Minor coastline where he honored the heroes of the Trojan War.
In commemoration of the victory Alexander sent 300 Persian shields which were hung in Parthenon.
He granted full self-rule to the Ionian cities.
Furthermore, the mass numbersof the Persian army are mentioned in the writings of Arrianos.

Page 64: The mausoleum of Alicarnassos (one of the 7 wonders). Its height reached 55 meters and its architects were Pythios and Styros (it was made by Leocharis, Skopas, Timotheos, Vryaxis).

Page 65: In the big icon the wonderful temple of Apollo (didimeo) is shown. The height of the pillars was 15,45 meters (8X21) (a 6th century B.C construction). The temple had been subject to damages by the Persians. Alexander gave money for the construction of a new temple with colossal dimensions. The height of the pillars was 19,70 meters (10X21 pillars). Its architects were Peonios and Dafnis.

Page 71: Alexander the Great together with his soldiers traveled in 8.5 years over 18.000 kms. This is a gigantic achievement and exceeds by far the exploits of all other troops.

Page 73: There were a lot of libraries during the Hellenistic period. The greatest was the one in Alexandria which preserved 700.000 volumes. The Hellenistic states had been involved in conflicts amongnst themselves and wars.

BIBLIOGRAPHY

ΧΕΡΜΑΝ ΜΠΕΝΓΚΤΣΟΝ, ΙΣΤΟΡΙΑ ΤΗΣ ΑΡΧΑΙΑΣ ΕΛΛΑΔΟΣ
(από τις απαρχές μέχρι τη Ρωμαϊκή Αυτοκρατορία).
Εκδοτικός Οίκος "ΜΕΛΙΣΣΑ", Αθήνα 1979

ΜΑΝΟΛΗΣ ΑΝΔΡΟΝΙΚΟΣ, ΑΚΡΟΠΟΛΗ
ΕΚΔΟΤΙΚΗ ΑΘΗΝΩΝ Α.Ε., Αθήνα 2003

ΕΛΕΝΗ ΦΡΑΤΖΗ, Η Ακρόπολις
ΕΚΔΟΣΕΙΣ VOUTSAS EDITION

ΑΡΧΑΙΑ ΕΛΛΗΝΙΚΗ ΓΡΑΜΜΑΤΕΙΑ "ΟΙ ΕΛΛΗΝΕΣ"
ΠΛΟΥΤΑΡΧΟΣ, ΒΙΟΙ ΠΑΡΑΛΛΗΛΟΙ
(Σόλων, Μιλτιάδης, Θεμιστοκλής, Κίμων, Αριστείδης, Λύσανδρος, Τιμολέων, Αλέξανδρος).
ΕΚΔΟΣΕΙΣ ΚΑΚΤΟΣ, ΟΔΥΣΣΕΑΣ ΧΑΤΖΟΠΟΥΛΟΣ& ΣΙΑ Ο.Ε.

Ζαν Σαρμπάνο-Ρολάν
Μαρτέν-Φρανσουά Βιγιάρ, Ελλάδα
ΑΡΧΑΪΚΗ ΕΠΟΧΗ ΑΠΟ ΤΟΝ 7ο ΕΩΣ ΤΟΝ 5ο ΑΙΩΝΑ π.Χ.
ΚΛΑΣΙΚΗ ΕΠΟΧΗ ΑΠΟ ΤΟΝ 5ο ΕΩΣ ΤΟΝ 3ο ΑΙΩΝΑ π.Χ.
ΕΛΛΗΝΙΣΤΙΚΗ ΕΠΟΧΗ ΑΠΟ ΤΟΝ 3ο ΕΩΣ ΤΟΝ 1ο ΑΙΩΝΑ π.Χ.
Editions Gallimard, Paris, ΜΕΓΑΛΟΙ ΠΟΛΙΤΙΣΜΟΙ, Η ΚΑΘΗΜΕΡΙΝΗ

Η ΑΓΟΡΑ ΤΗΣ ΑΡΧΑΙΑΣ ΑΘΗΝΑΣ, ΣΥΝΤΟΜΟΣ ΟΔΗΓΟΣ
ΑΜΕΡΙΚΑΝΙΚΗ ΣΧΟΛΗ ΚΛΑΣΙΚΩΝ ΣΠΟΥΔΩΝ, ΑΘΗΝΑ 1985

Λουκία Θεοδώρου-Βασιλική Γκράτζιου, Βεργίνα
ΘΗΣΑΥΡΟΙ, ΜΥΘΟΙ ΚΑΙ ΙΣΤΟΡΙΑ ΤΗΣ ΜΑΚΕΔΟΝΙΚΗΣ ΓΗΣ
Εκδόσεις ΑΜΜΟΣ 1993

ΙΩΑΝΝΗΣ ΤΟΥΡΑΤΖΟΓΛΟΥ, ΜΑΚΕΔΟΝΙΑ, ΙΣΤΟΡΙΑ-ΜΝΗΜΕΙΑ, ΜΟΥΣΕΙΑ
ΕΚΔΟΤΙΚΗ ΑΘΗΝΩΝ, ΑΘΗΝΑ 1995

ΑΝΝΑ ΜΑΡΑΝΤΗ, ΔΕΛΦΟΙ, ΜΥΘΟΣ & ΙΣΤΟΡΙΑ -Ο ΑΡΧΑΙΟΛΟΓΙΚΟΣ ΧΩΡΟΣ- ΤΟ ΜΟΥΣΕΙΟ
ΕΚΔΟΣΕΙΣ Μ.ΤΟΥΜΠΗΣ Α.Ε., ΑΘΗΝΑ 2000

Γ. ΚΟΚΚΟΡΟΥ-ΑΛΕΥΡΑ, Η ΤΕΧΝΗ ΤΗΣ ΑΡΧΑΙΑΣ ΕΛΛΑΔΑΣ, ΣΥΝΤΟΜΗ ΙΣΤΟΡΙΑ (1050-50π.Χ.)
ΕΚΔΟΣΕΙΣ ΚΑΡΔΑΜΙΤΣΑ, ΑΘΗΝΑ 1995

ΝΙΚΟΥ ΠΑΠΑΧΑΤΖΗ, ΜΥΚΗΝΕΣ-ΕΠΙΔΑΥΡΟΣ-ΤΙΡΥΝΘΑ-ΝΑΥΠΛΙΟ-
ΗΡΑΙΟ ΤΟΥ ΑΡΓΟΥΣ-ΑΡΓΟΣ-ΑΣΙΝΗ-ΛΕΡΝΑ-ΤΡΟΙΖΗΝΙΑ
ΕΚΔΟΣΕΙΣ ΚΛΕΙΩ, ΑΘΗΝΑ 1986

ALEXANDER FARNOUX
Knossos, Unearthing a Legend
NEW HORIZONS-THAMES AND HUDSON

ΧΡΗΣΤΟΣ Γ. ΝΤΟΥΜΑΣ, Σαντορίνη
Η ΠΡΟΪΣΤΟΡΙΚΗ ΠΟΛΗ ΤΟΥ ΑΚΡΩΤΗΡΙΟΥ
ΕΚΔΟΤΙΚΟΣ ΟΙΚΟΣ HANNIBAL, ΑΘΗΝΑ

Απόστολος Ε. Βακαλόπουλος
Νέα Ελληνική Ιστορία 1904-1985
ΕΚΔΟΣΕΙΣ ΒΑΝΙΑΣ, ΘΕΣΣΑΛΟΝΙΚΗ 1988

ΠΑΓΚΟΣΜΙΑ ΕΙΚΟΝΟΓΡΑΦΗΜΕΝΗ ΕΝΔΥΜΑΤΟΛΟΓΙΑ
5000 ΧΡΟΝΙΑ ΙΣΤΟΡΙΑ ΜΟΔΑΣ
ΟΡΓΑΝΙΣΜΟΣ ΔΗΜΗΤΡΕΛΗ, ΘΕΣΣΑΛΟΝΙΚΗ

CPSIA information can be obtained at www.ICGtesting.com
Printed in the USA
LVIW01n1441040216
473699LV00018B/107